# AWESOME
# MACHINES
## COLORING & ACTIVITY BOOK

BENDON™

© 2010
Bendon Publishing International, Inc.
Ashland, OH 44805
www.bendonpub.com

# DECODE the secret message.

1=A
2=B
3=C
4=D
5=E
6=F
7=G
8=H
9=I
10=J
11=K
12=L
13=M
14=N
15=O
16=P
17=Q
18=R
19=S
20=T
21=U
22=V
23=W
24=X
25=Y
26=Z

$\underline{\phantom{4}}$ $\underline{\phantom{9}}$ $\underline{\phantom{18}}$ $\underline{\phantom{20}}$
4   9   18   20

$\underline{\phantom{2}}$ $\underline{\phantom{9}}$ $\underline{\phantom{11}}$ $\underline{\phantom{5}}$ $\underline{\phantom{19}}$
2   9   11   5   19

$\underline{\phantom{7}}$ $\underline{\phantom{15}}$ $\underline{\phantom{6}}$ $\underline{\phantom{1}}$ $\underline{\phantom{19}}$ $\underline{\phantom{20}}$
7   15   6   1   19   20

# DRAW a spaceship in outer space.

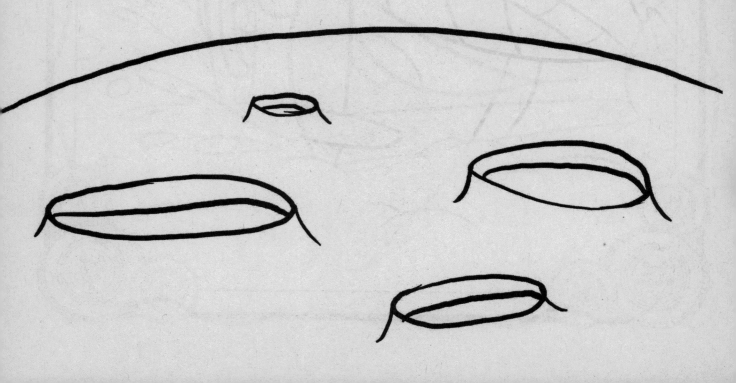

# COUNT the space ships.

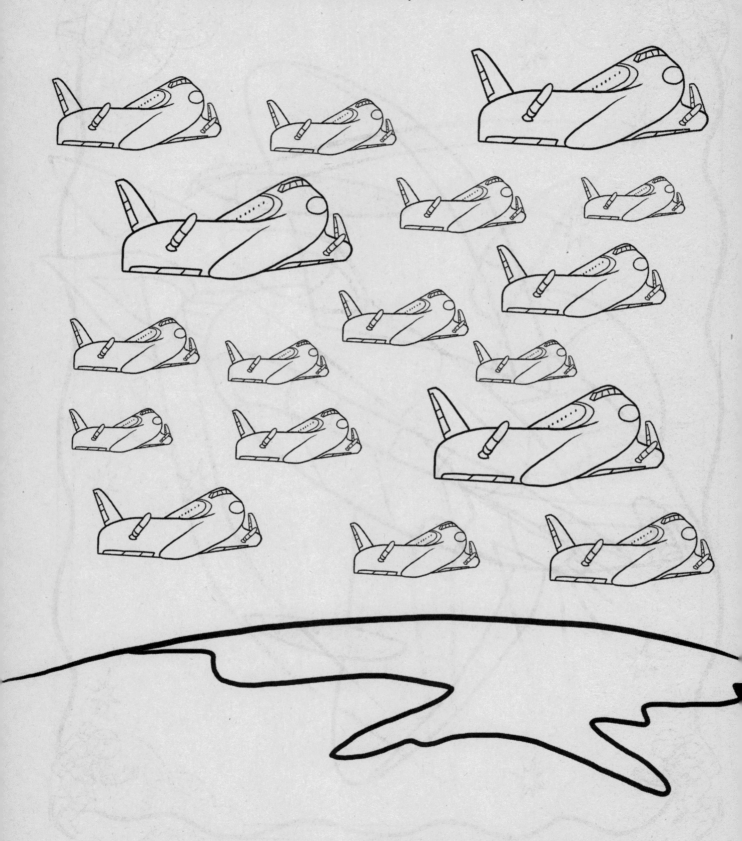

# Circle the picture that is **DIFFERENT**.

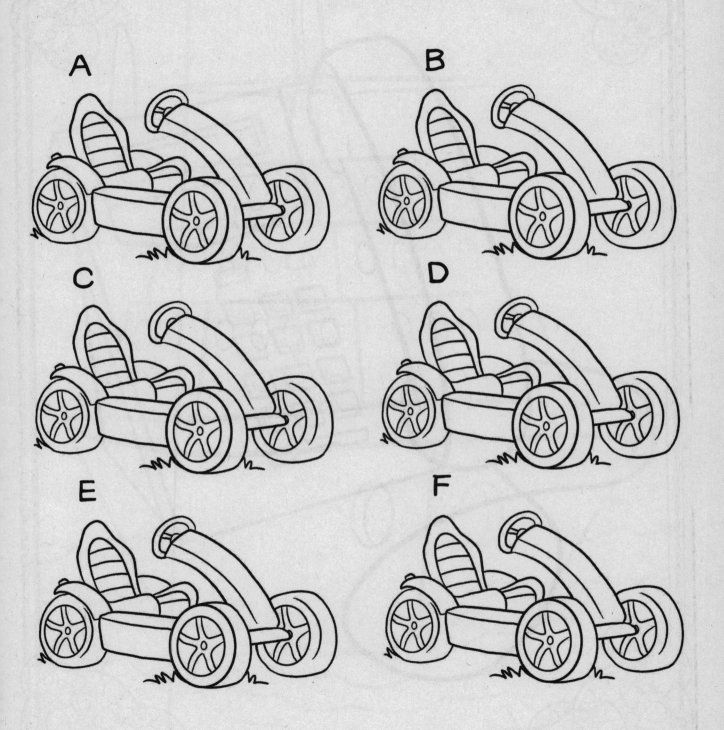

A

B

C

D

E

F

# Connect the dots.

Use the grid
to help you
**DRAW**
the picture!

# Use the grid to **DRAW** the other half of the picture.

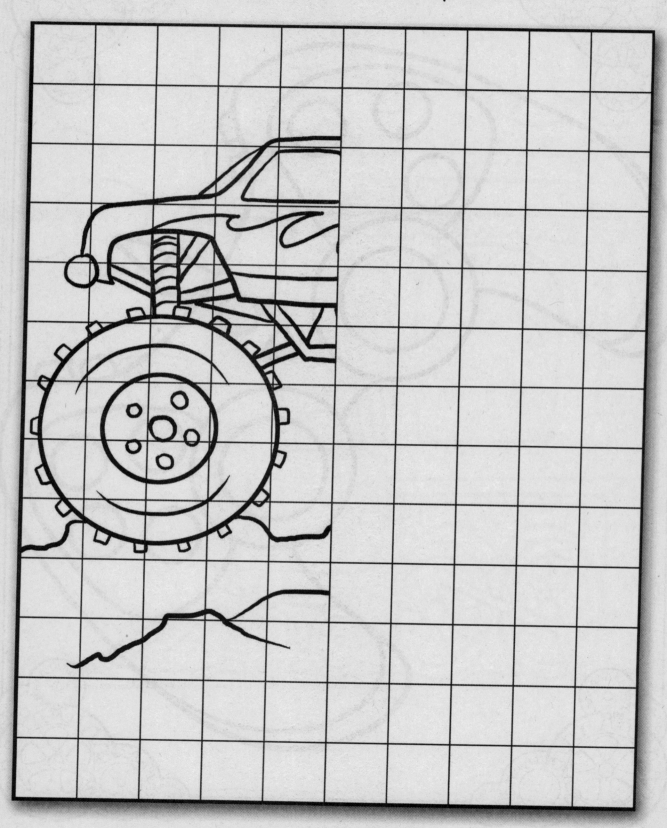

How many words can you
think of using the letters in:

# OFF ROAD
# VEHICLE

_____

_____

_____

_____

_____

_____

_____

_____

_____

# Draw a line to the images that **MATCH**.

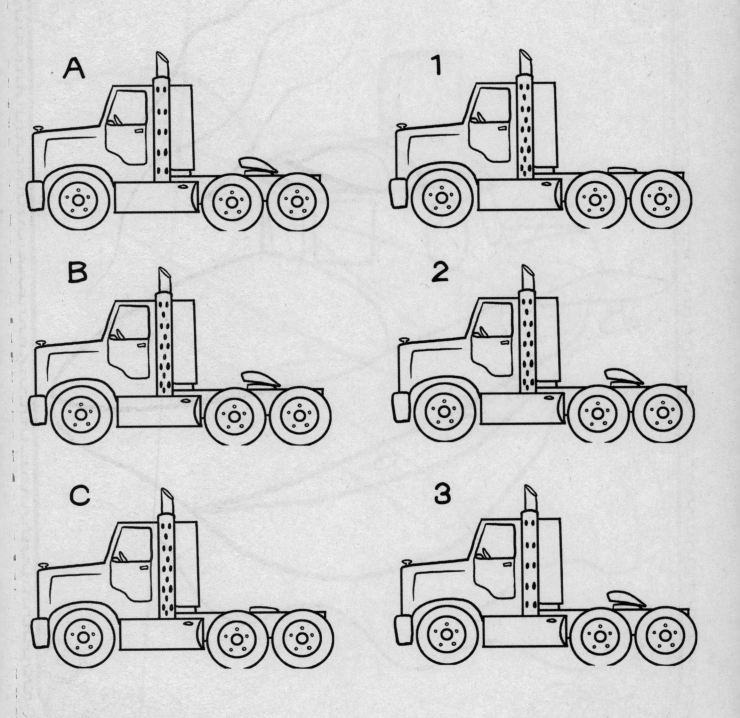

A

B

C

1

2

3

# Solve the MAZE

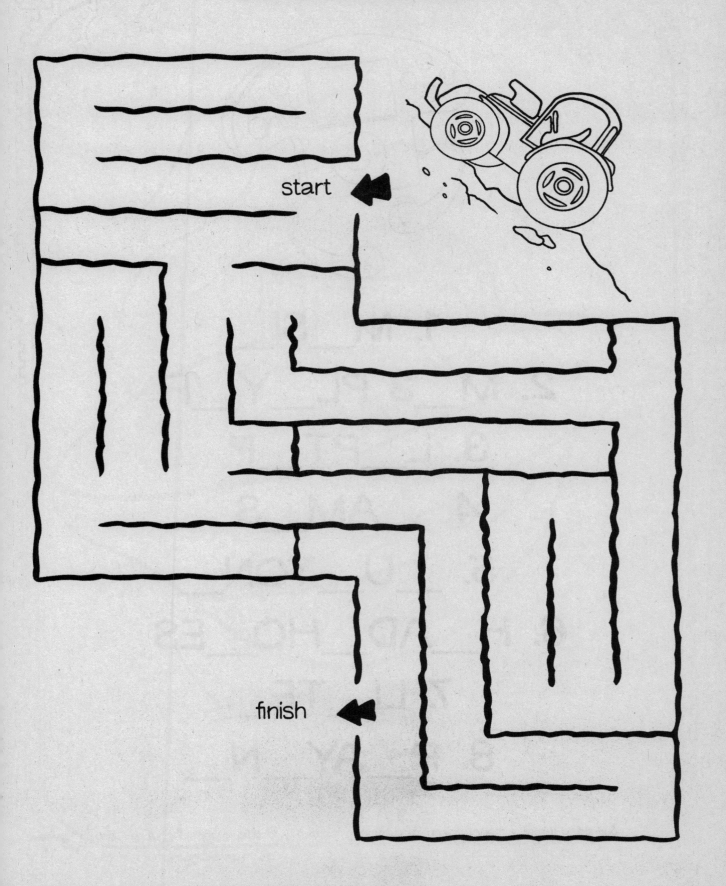

# FILL IN the missing letters.

1. M__SI__

2. M__3 PL__Y__R

3. L__PT__P

4. __AM__S

5. __U__TON__

6. H__AD__HO__ES

7. LI__TE__

8. P__AY__N__

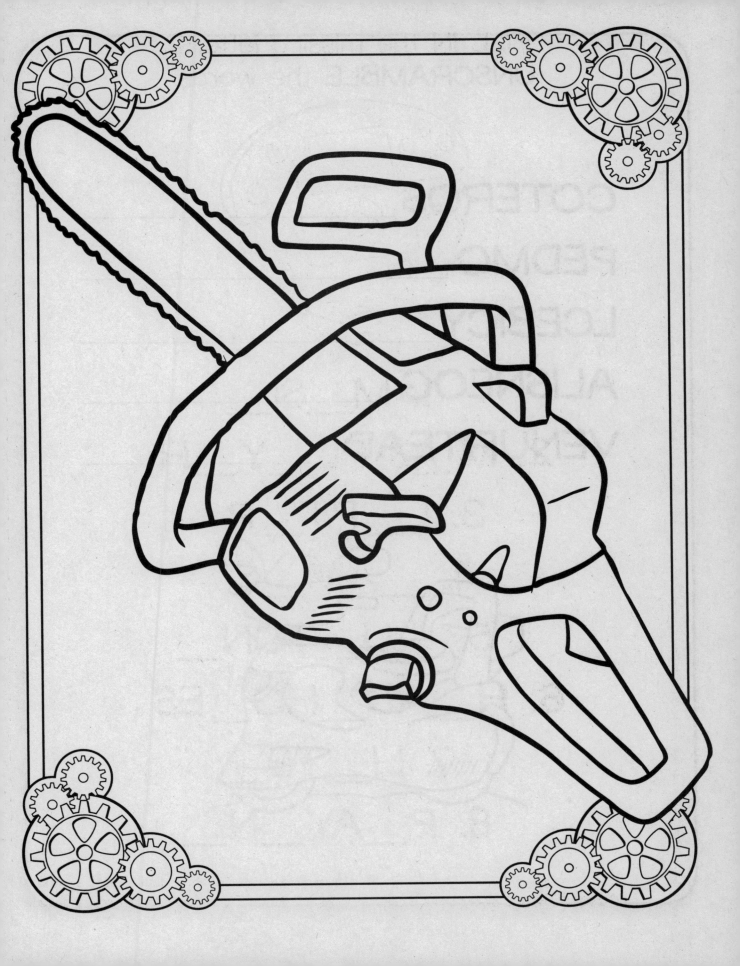

# UNSCRAMBLE the words.

COTEROS _____

PEDMO _____

LCEBICY _____

ALISNEOG _____

VENURTEAD _____

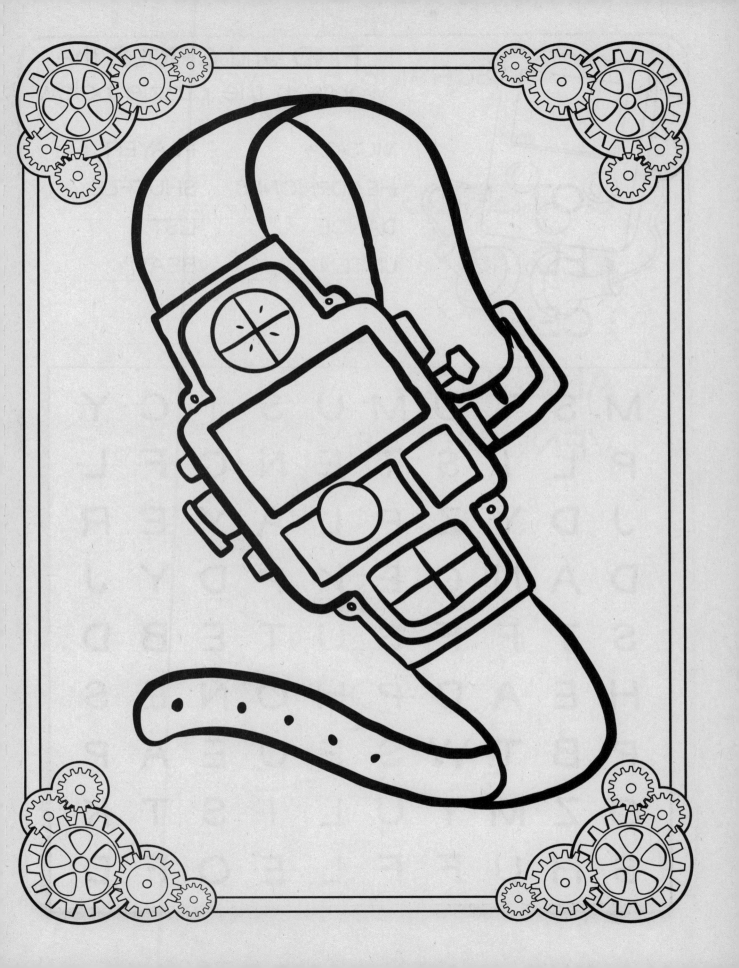

# FIND and CIRCLE the words in the puzzle below:

MUSIC          PLAYER

HEADPHONES     SHUFFLE

DANCE          LIST

LISTEN         BEAT

```
M S T U M U S I C Y
P L I S T E N C F L
J D Y Z P L A Y E R
D A N C E K P D Y J
S T F F S U T E B D
H E A D P H O N E S
P B T W S E U E A P
O Z M Y U L I S T K
S H U F F L E O F D
```

# DECODE the secret message.

1=A
2=B
3=C
4=D
5=E
6=F
7=G
8=H
9=I
10=J
11=K
12=L
13=M
14=N
15=O
16=P
17=Q
18=R
19=S
20=T
21=U
22=V
23=W
24=X
25=Y
26=Z

__ __ __ __ __ __ __
5  24  16  12  15  18  5

__ __ __ __ __
15  21  20  5  18

__ __ __ __ __
19  16  1  3  5

# What is the crane lifting?
## DRAW its load.

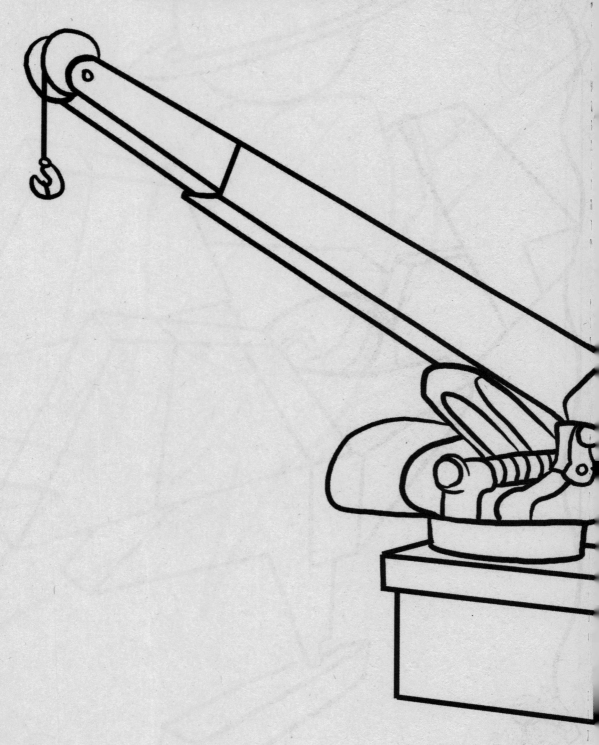

# COUNT the drills.

# Circle the picture that is DIFFERENT.

A            B

C            D

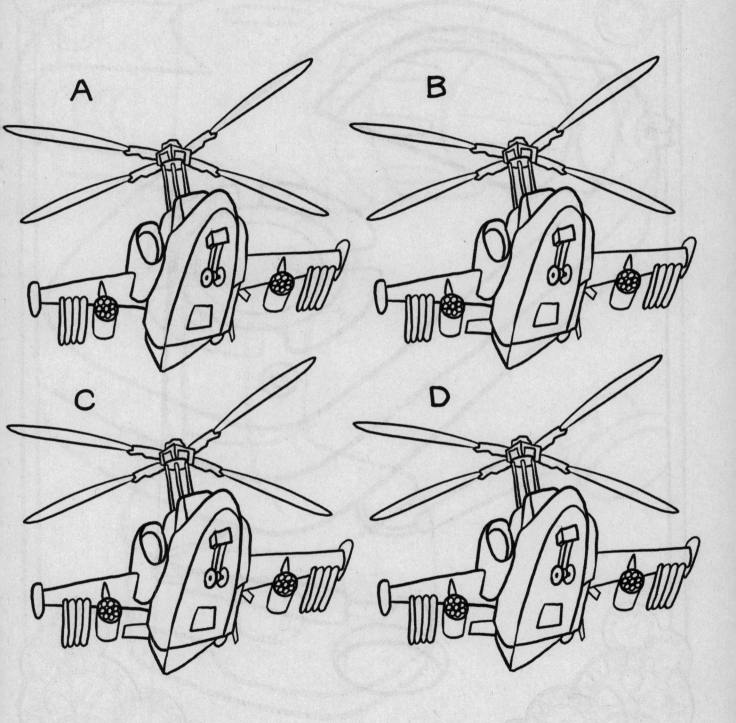

# Connect the dots.

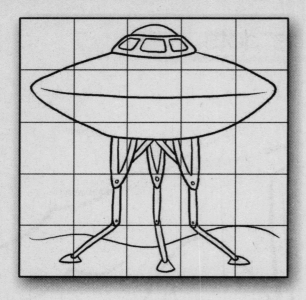

Use the grid
to help you
**DRAW**
the picture!

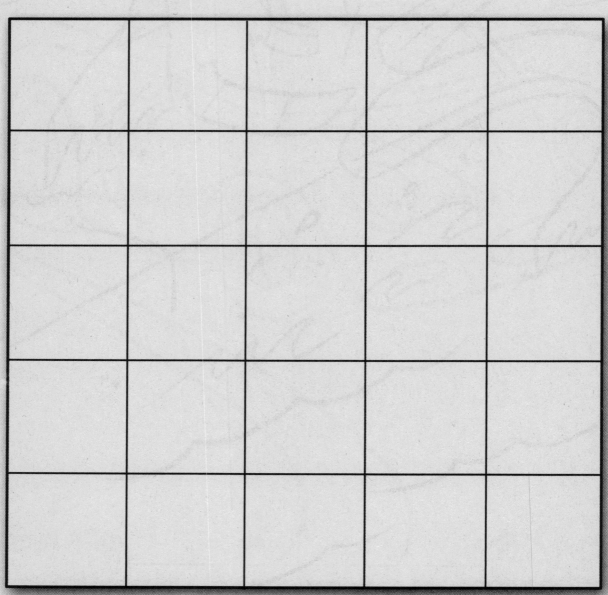

# Use the grid to **DRAW** the other half of the picture.

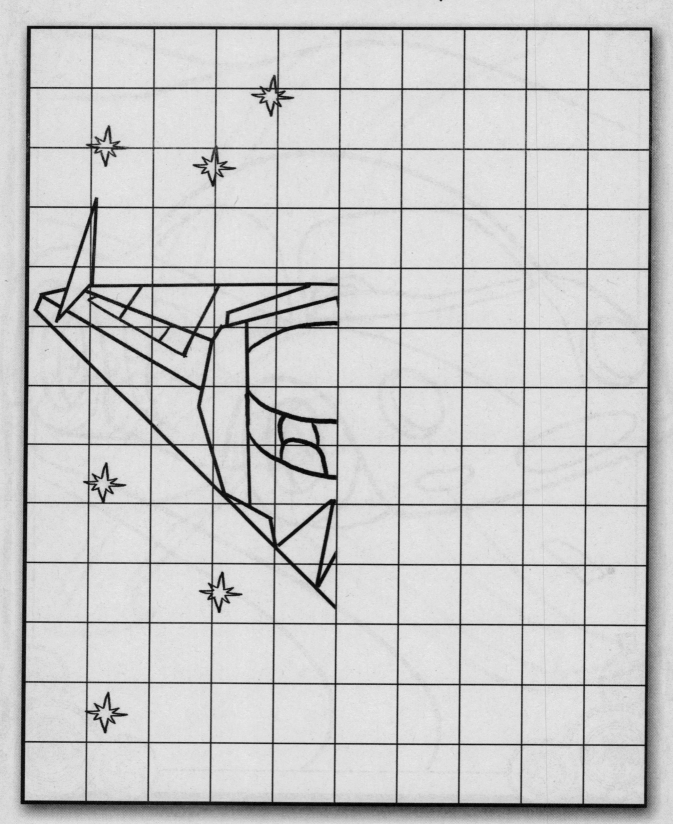

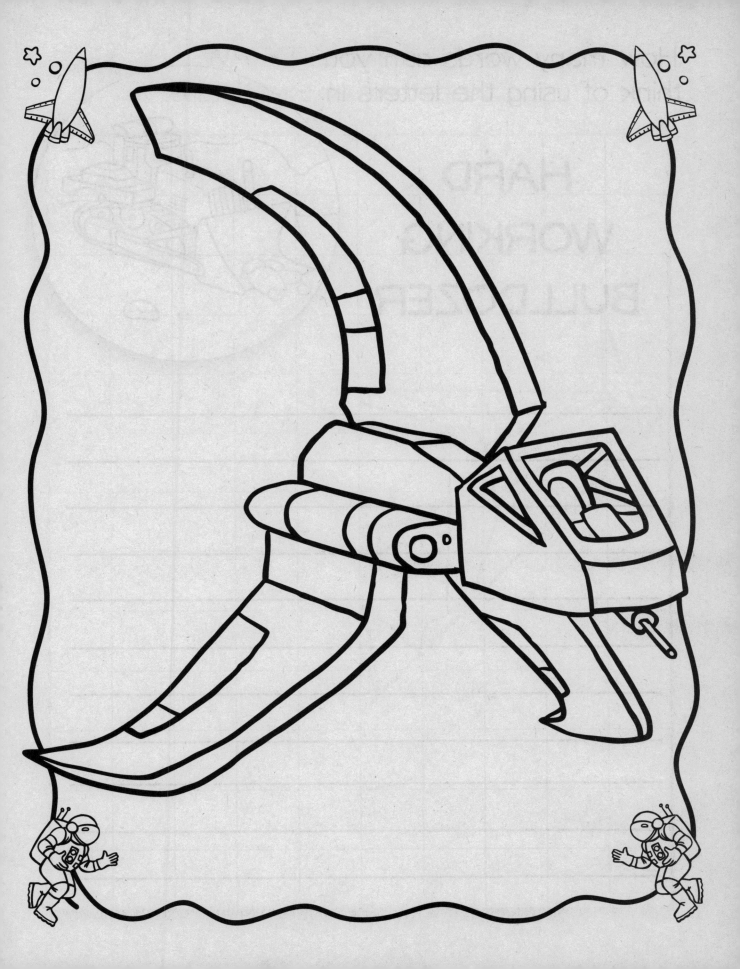

How many words can you
think of using the letters in:

# HARD
# WORKING
# BULLDOZER

_____

_____

_____

_____

_____

_____

_____

_____

# Draw a line to the images that **MATCH.**

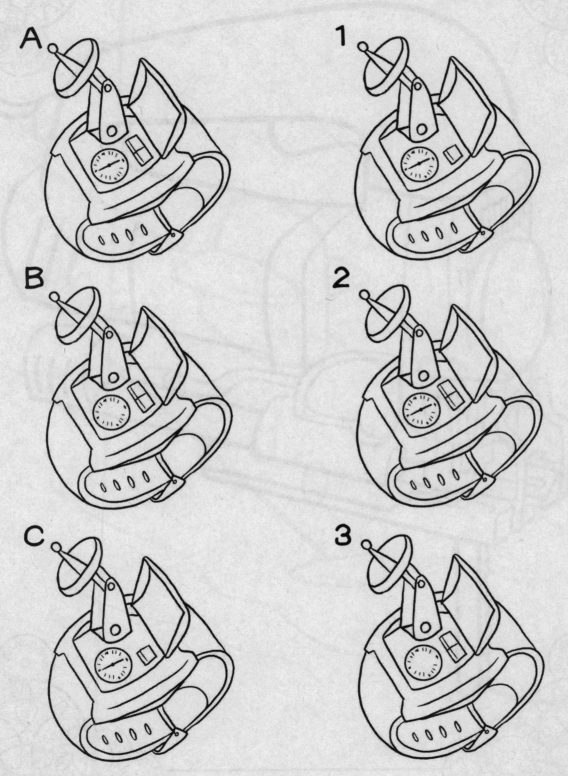

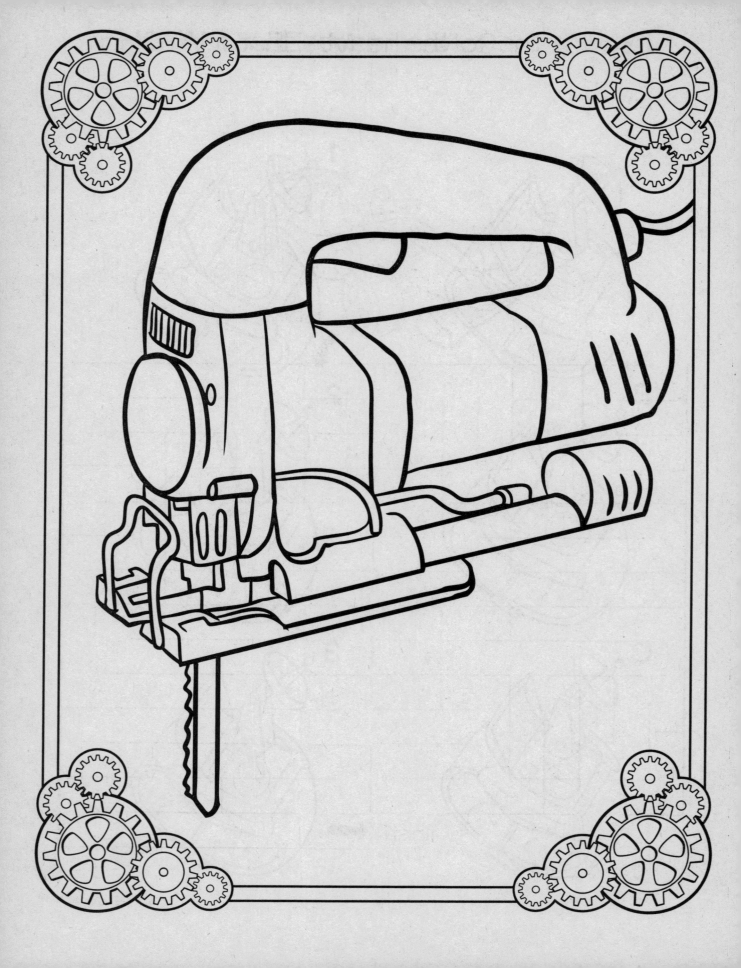

# Solve the MAZE

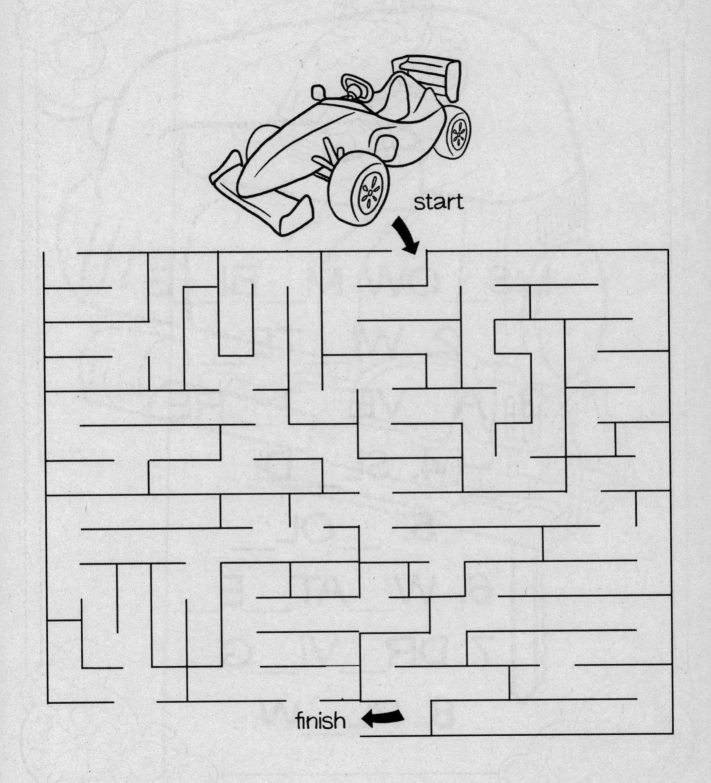

start

finish

# FILL IN the missing letters.

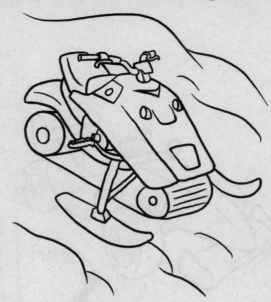

1. S__OW M__BI__E

2. WI__TE__

3. A__VE__T__RE

4. SL__D

5. __OL__

6. W__AT__E__

7. DR__VI__G

8. PL__W

# UNSCRAMBLE the words.

GIB IGR _____

CRUKT _____

VELRTA _____

STNADICE _____

GORAC _____

# FIND and CIRCLE the words in the puzzle below:

| | |
|---|---|
| TRUCK | DUMP |
| GARBAGE | RECYCLE |
| LOAD | CARRY |
| TRANSPORT | LIFT |

```
T R U C K L K A V T
R K O L T J C E D H
A M G A R B A G E T
N E F I E D R E O L
S B V Q O T R G I I
P N M G L B Y M T F
O D U M P D F I Y T
R E C Y C L E U R R
T Y J E R T L O A D
```

# DECODE the secret message.

1=A
2=B
3=C
4=D
5=E
6=F
7=G
8=H
9=I
10=J
11=K
12=L
13=M
14=N
15=O
16=P
17=Q
18=R
19=S
20=T
21=U
22=V
23=W
24=X
25=Y
26=Z

ICE CREAM

__ __ __ __ __ ,
23  8  1  20 19

__ __ __ __
25 15 21 18

__ __ __ __ __ __ __ __
6  1  22 15 18 9  20 5

__ __ __  __ __ __ __ __ ?
9  3  5   3  18 5  1  13

This bulldozer is hard at work.
**DRAW** the construction site.

# COUNT the planets.

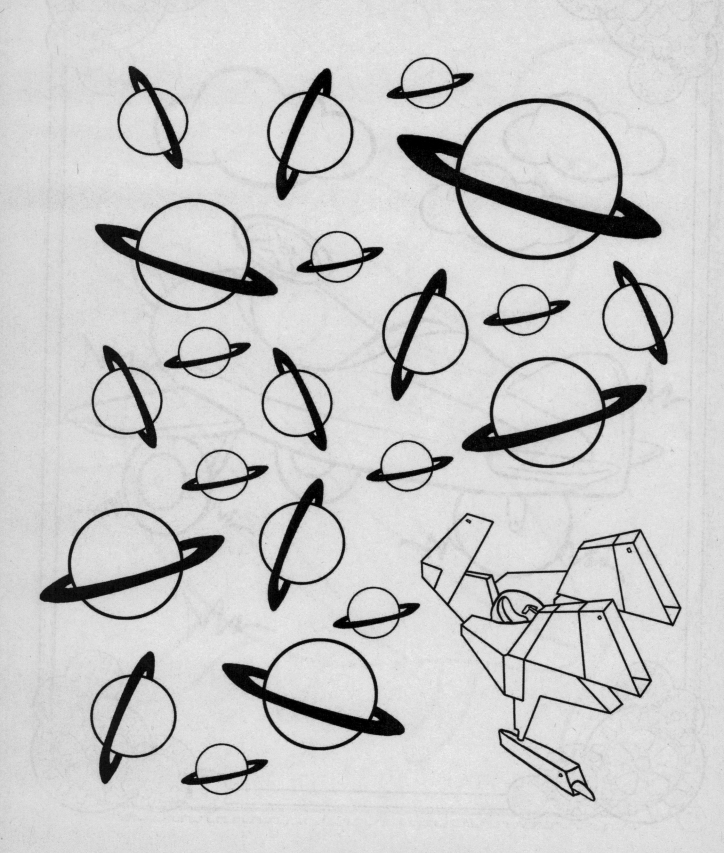

# Circle the picture that is DIFFERENT.

A

B

C

D

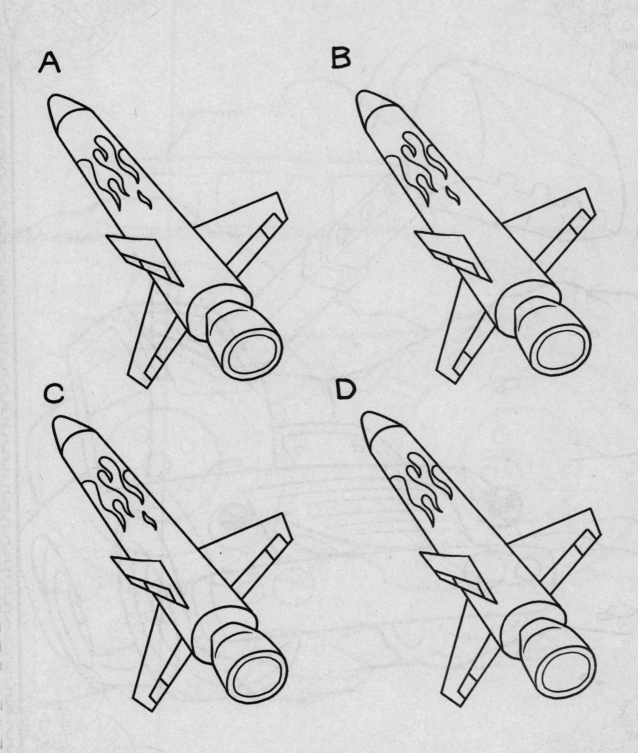

# Connect the dots.

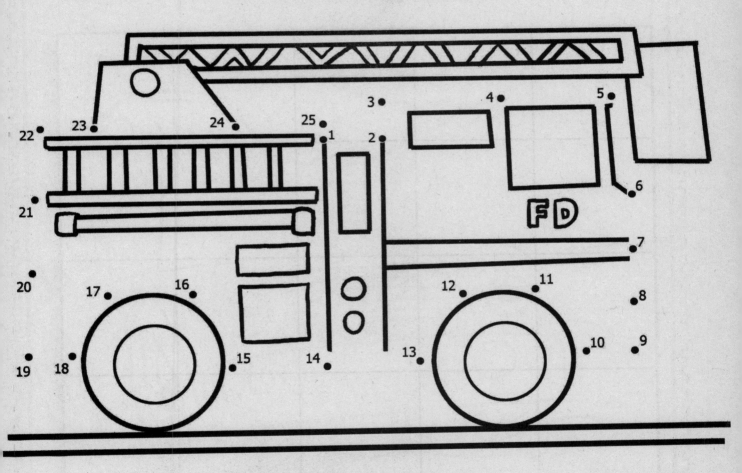

Use the grid
to help you
**DRAW**
the picture!

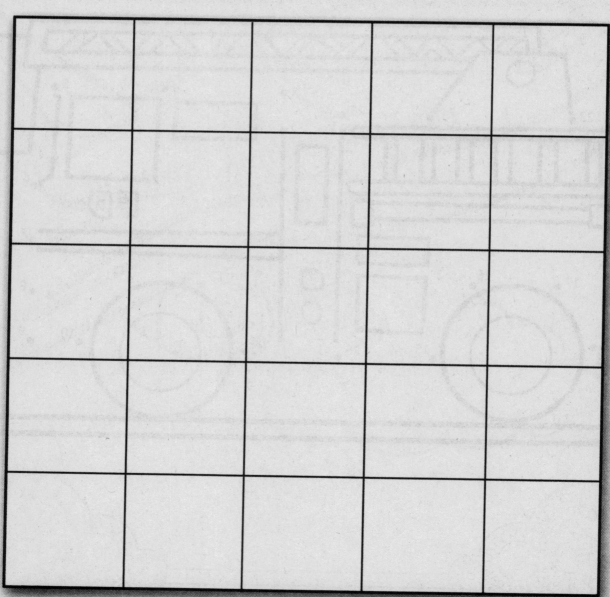

# Use the grid to DRAW
## the other half of the picture.

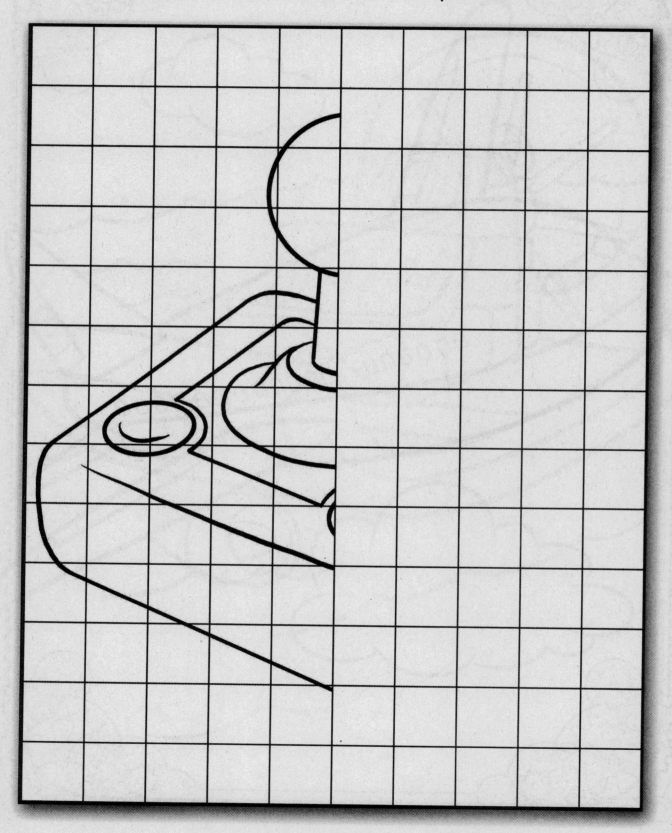

How many words can you
think of using the letters in:

## GO KART
## RACES

_____

_____

_____

_____

_____

_____

_____

_____

_____

# Draw a line to the images that **MATCH**.

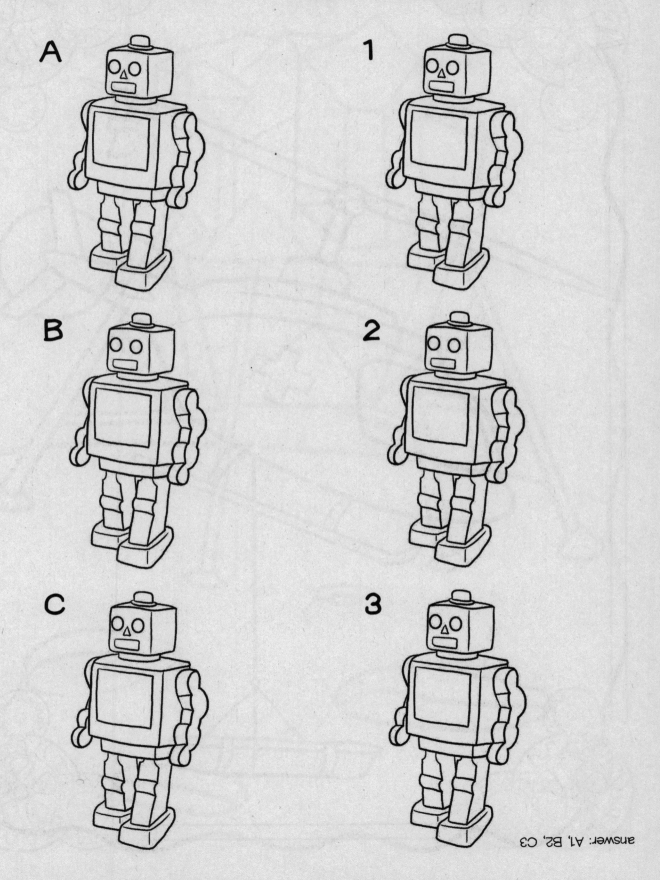

A

B

C

1

2

3

answer: A1, B2, C3

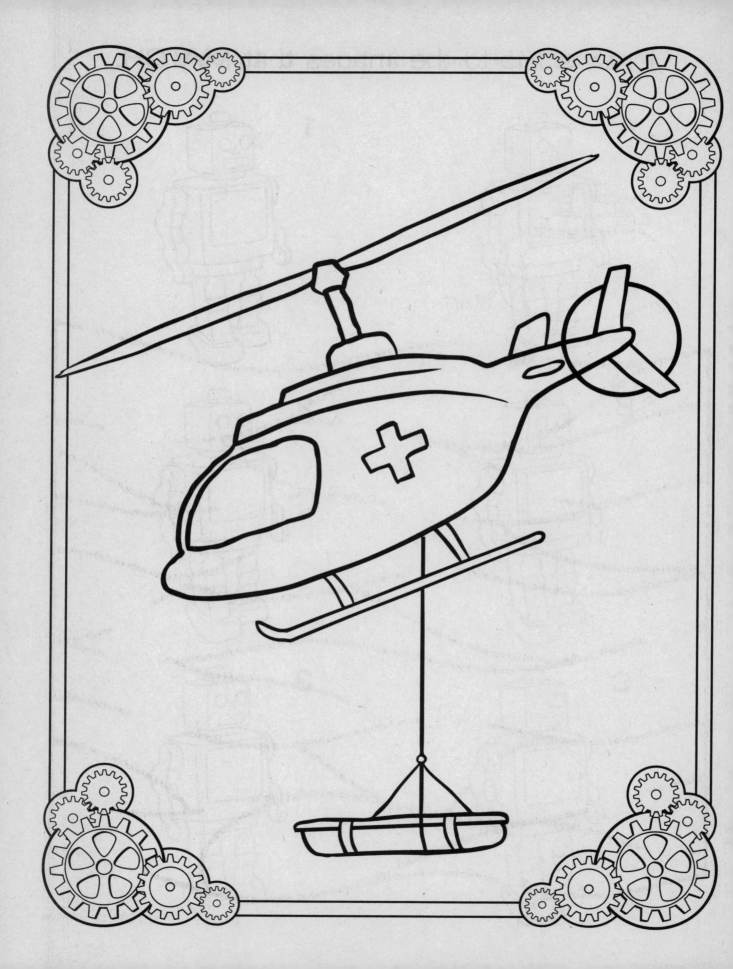

# Help the submarine find its way.

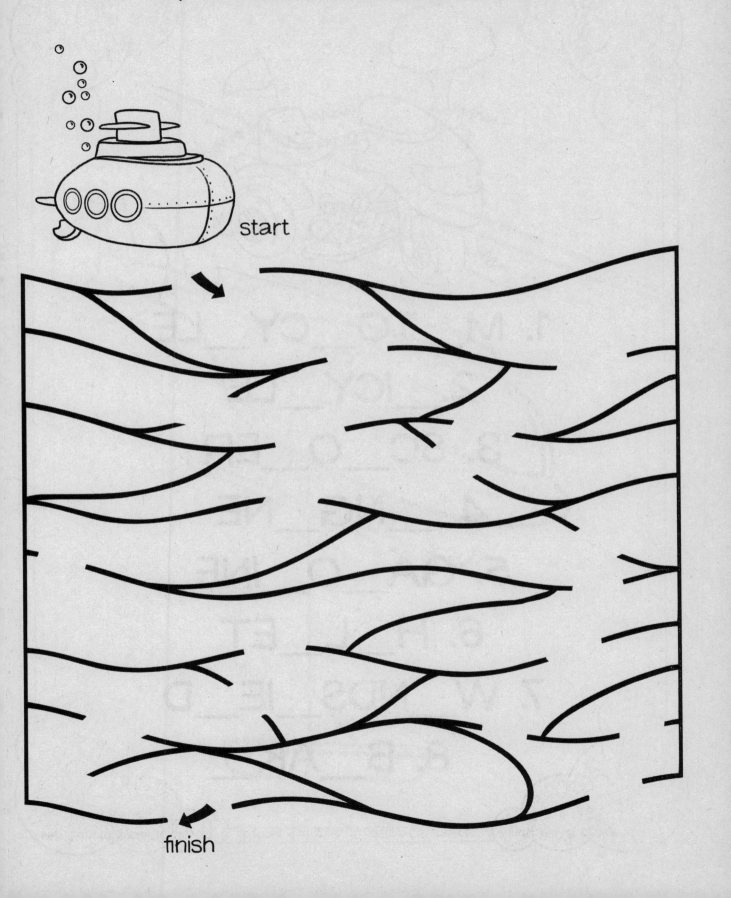

start

finish

# FILL IN the missing letters.

1. M_ _TO_ _CY_ _LE

2. _ _ICY_ _LE

3. SC_ _O_ _ER

4. _ _NG_ _NE

5. GA_ _O_ _INE

6. H_ _L_ _ET

7. W_ _NDS_ _IE_ _D

8. B_ _AK_ _

# UNSCRAMBLE the words.

NEMCET _____

KRWO _____

STRUCNOCIONT _____

XIMNIG _____

BLDIU _____

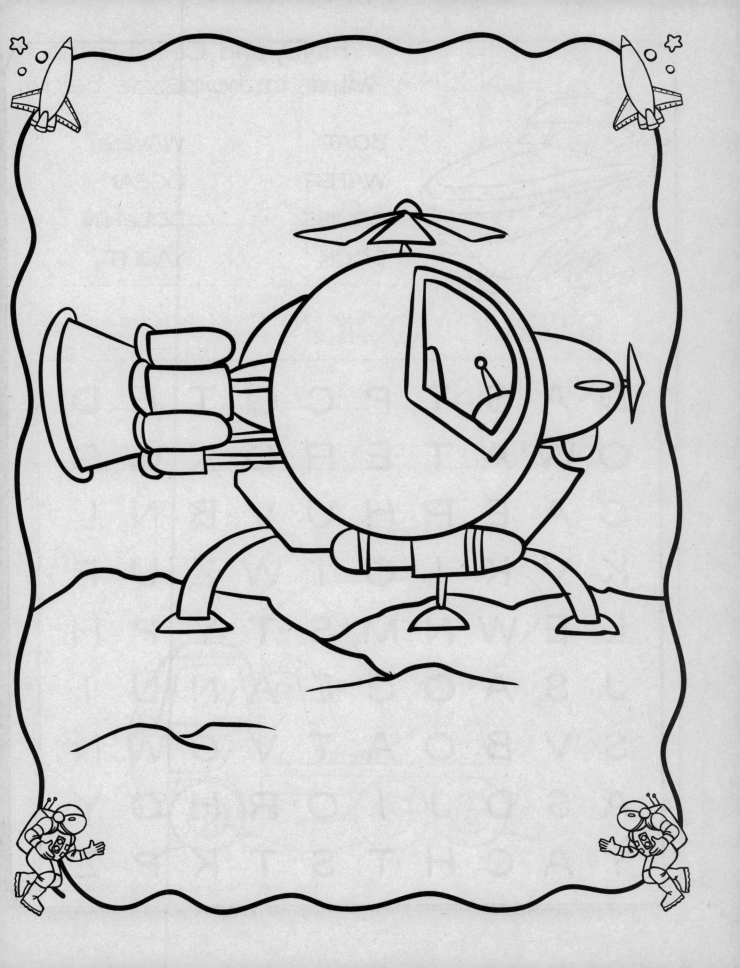

# FIND and CIRCLE the words in the puzzle below:

| | |
|---|---|
| BOAT | WAVES |
| WATER | OCEAN |
| CRUISE | DOLPHIN |
| DOCK | YACHT |

```
D A S T P C G T F D
O W A T E R O K W O
C A E R H U V B N L
K V K I O I W Z U P
L E W N M S T Y P H
J S A O C E A N U I
S V B O A T V C W N
A S D J I O R H O Y
Y A C H T S T K P Z
```

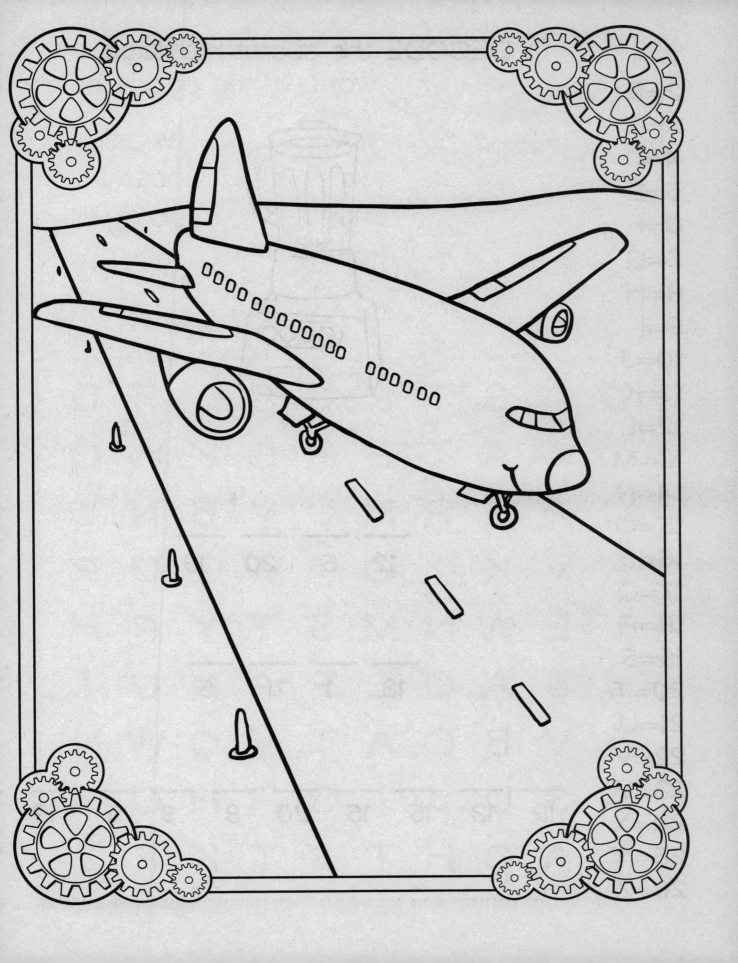

# DECODE the secret message.

1=A
2=B
3=C
4=D
5=E
6=F
7=G
8=H
9=I
10=J
11=K
12=L
13=M
14=N
15=O
16=P
17=Q
18=R
19=S
20=T
21=U
22=V
23=W
24=X
25=Y
26=Z

,

__ __ __ __
12  5  20  19

__ __ __ __
13  1  11  5

__ __ __ __ __ __ __ __ __
19 13 15 15 20  8  9  5 19

# DRAW a boat zooming through the waves!

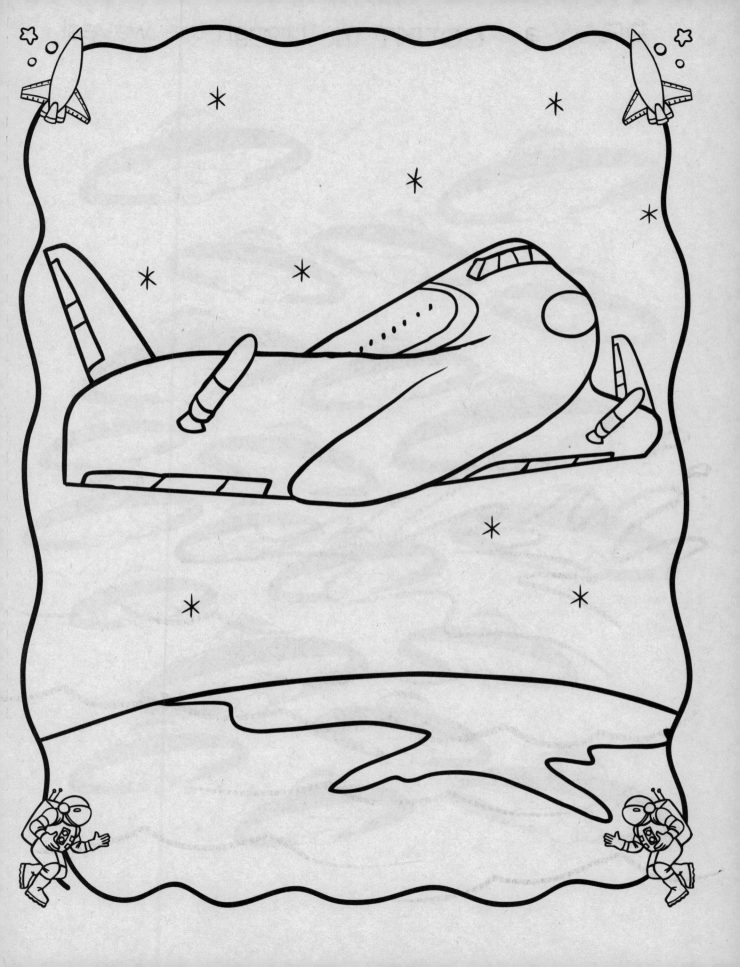

# COUNT the UFOs.

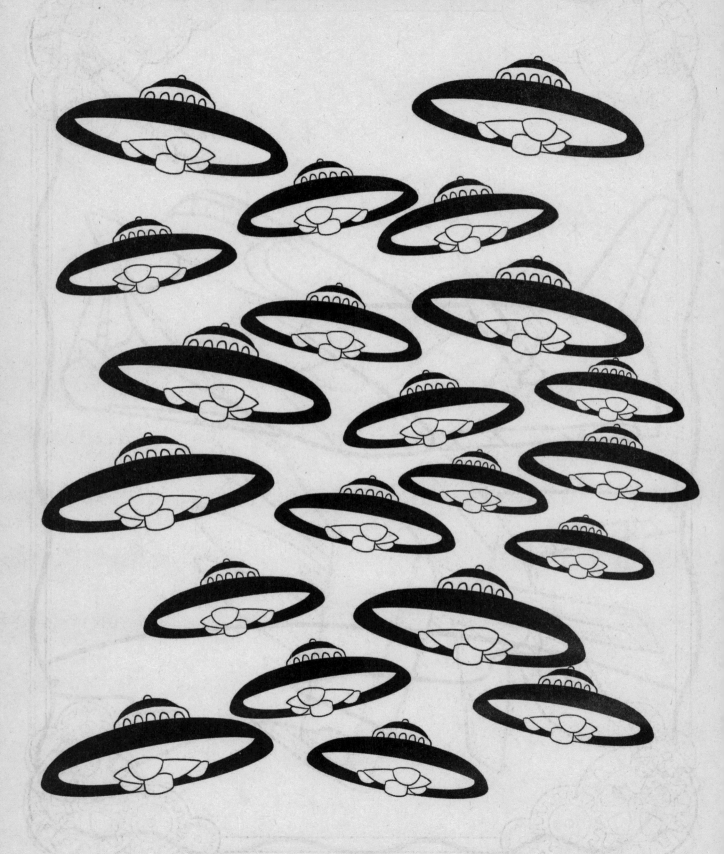

# Circle the picture that is **DIFFERENT**.

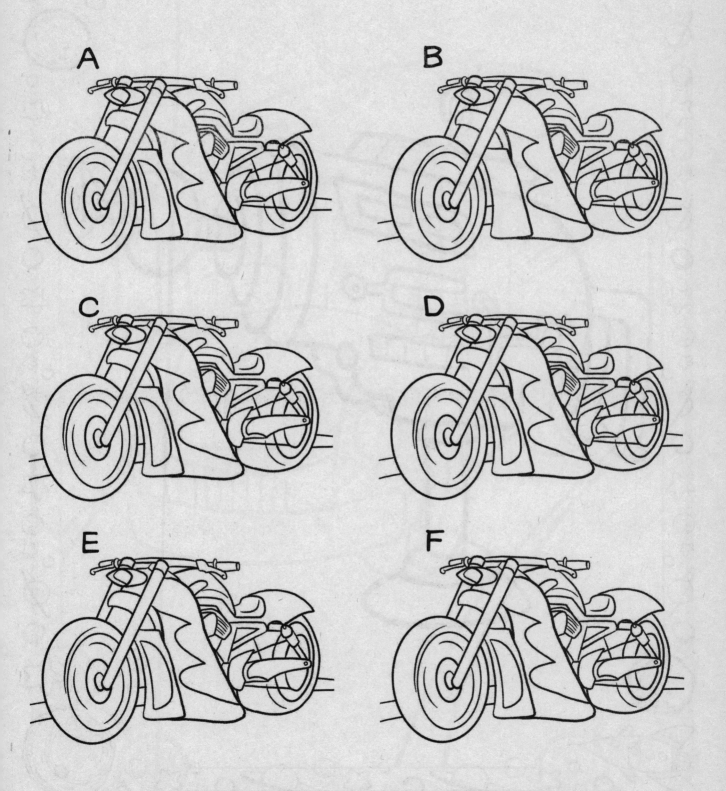

A

B

C

D

E

F

# Connect the dots.

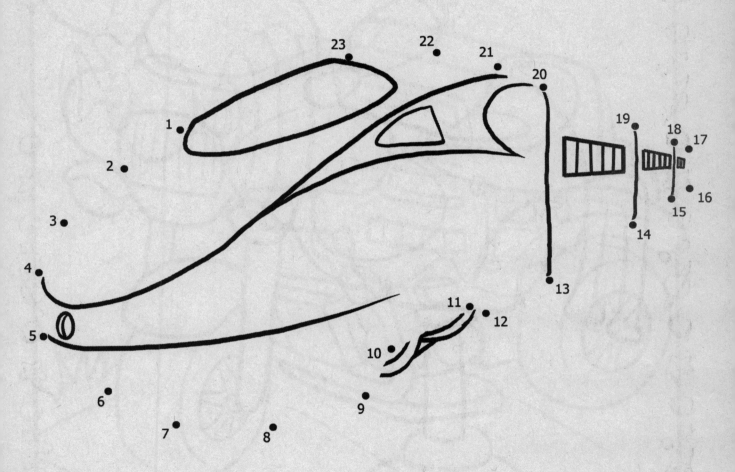

Use the grid
to help you
**DRAW**
the picture!

# Use the grid to DRAW
## the other half of the picture.

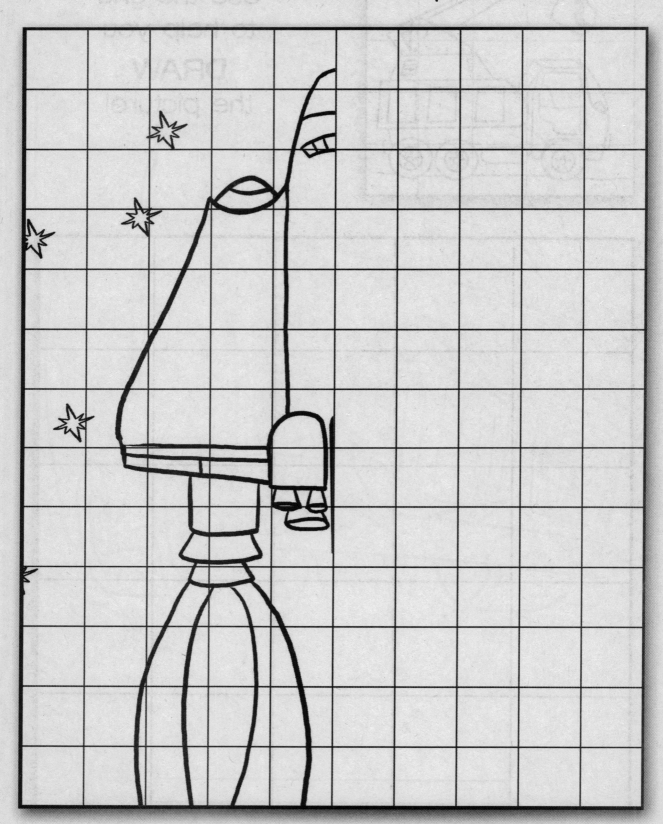

How many words can you
think of using the letters in:

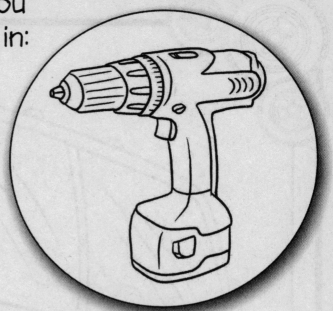

# HANDY MAN
# AT WORK

_____

_____

_____

_____

_____

_____

_____

_____

_____

# Draw a line to the images that MATCH.

# Which path wins the race?

finish

# FILL IN the missing letters.

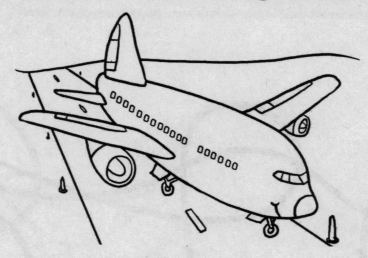

1. AI__PL__N__

2. R__N__AY

3. __R__VEL

4. V__CA__I__N

5. F__YI__G

6. __IN__S

7. T__K__O__F

8. __IRP__RT

# UNSCRAMBLE the words.

WALN _____

WOMER _____

YDAR _____

SRAGS _____

SELFMA _____

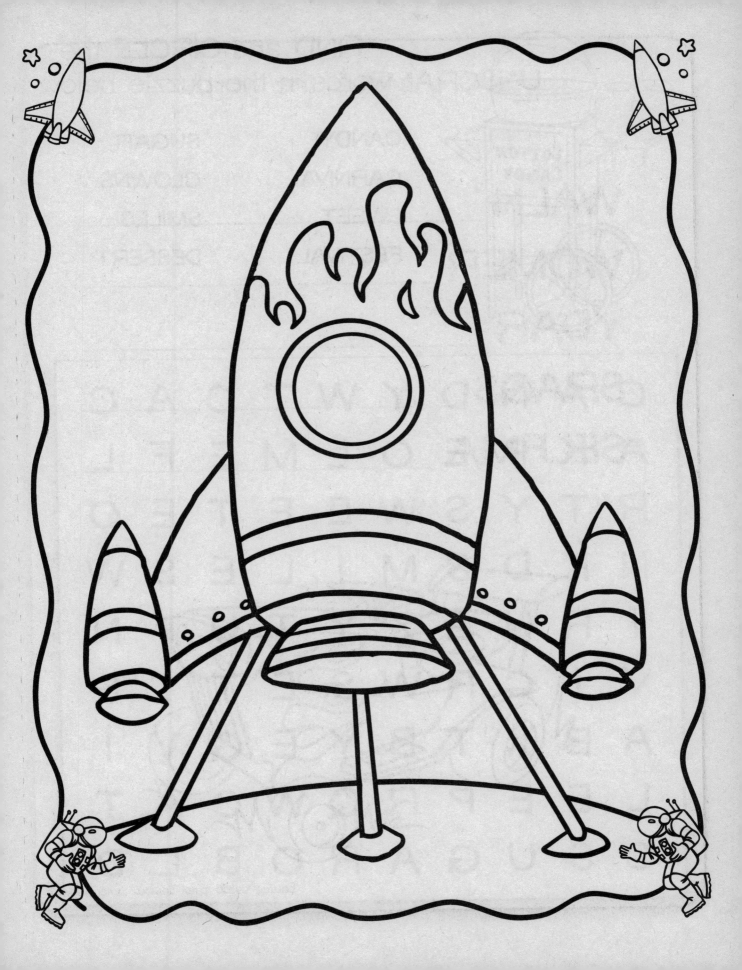

Cotton Candy

**FIND** and **CIRCLE** the words in the puzzle below:

CANDY          SUGAR

CARNIVAL       CLOWNS

SWEET          SMILES

FESTIVAL       DESSERT

```
C A N D Y W T C A C
A K P E O L M E F L
R T Y S W E E T E O
N K D S M I L E S W
I R U E Z Y T U T N
V I C R W S E T I S
A P X T B Y E G V I
L E E P R Q W C A T
C S U G A R O B L D
```

# DECODE the secret message.

1=A
2=B
3=C
4=D
5=E
6=F
7=G
8=H
9=I
10=J
11=K
12=L
13=M
14=N
15=O
16=P
17=Q
18=R
19=S
20=T
21=U
22=V
23=W
24=X
25=Y
26=Z

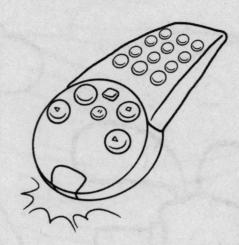

__ __ __ __ __ __
3  8  1  14  7  5

__ __ __
20  8  5

__ __ __ __ __ __ __
3  8  1  14  14  5  12

# DRAW an airplane flying through the clouds!

# COUNT the rocket ships.

# Circle the picture that is DIFFERENT.

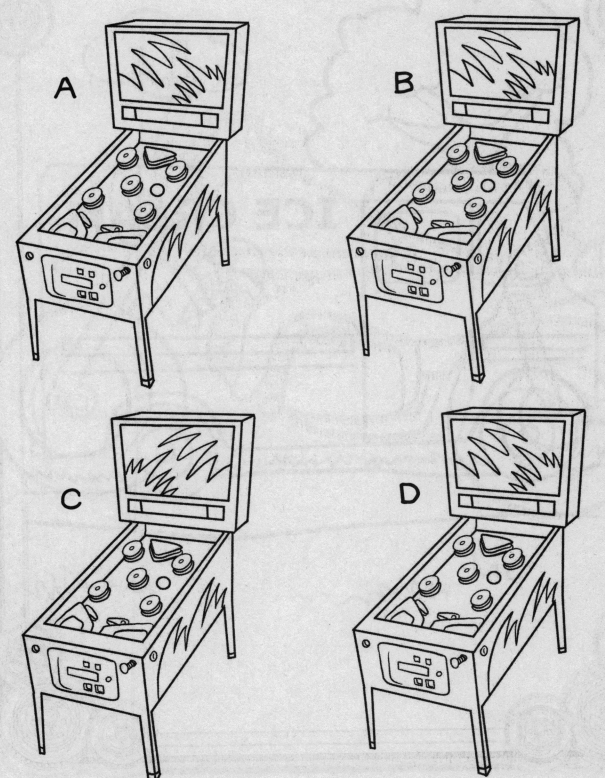

ICE CREAM

# Connect the dots.

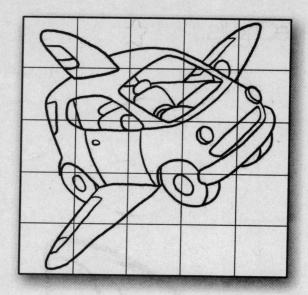

Use the grid
to help you
**DRAW**
the picture!

# Use the grid to **DRAW** the other half of the picture.

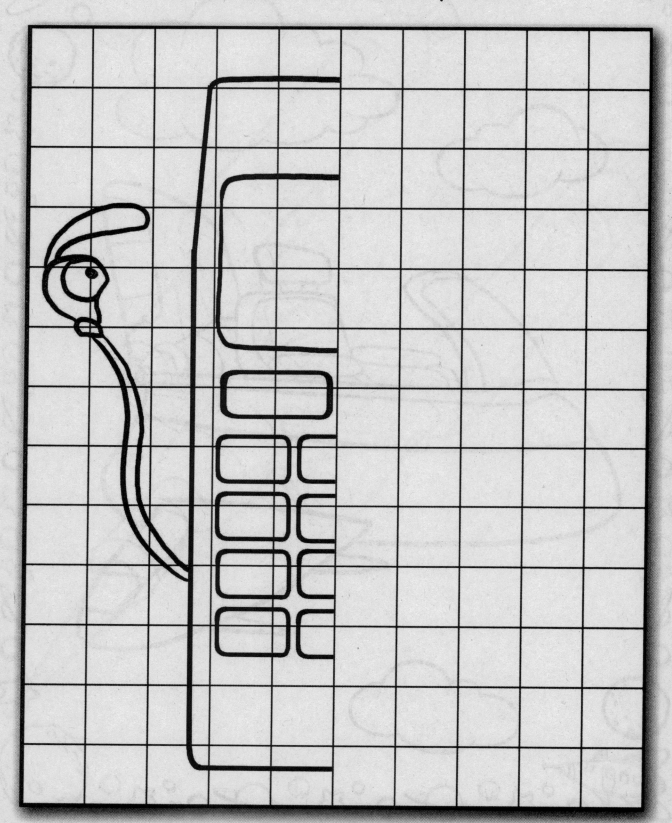

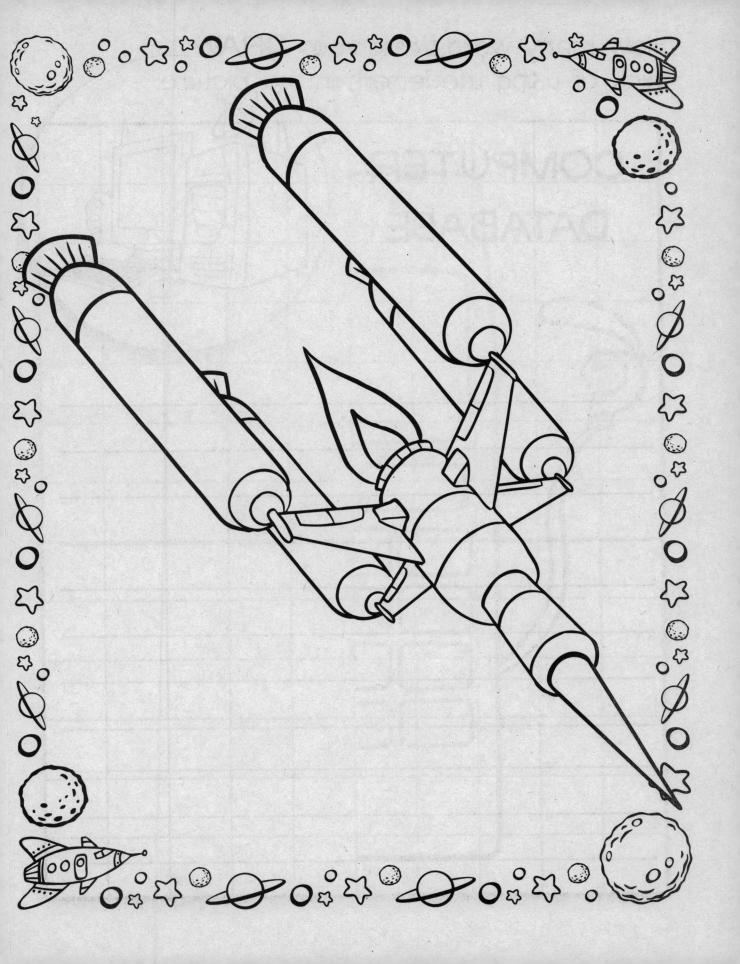

How many words can you
think of using the letters in:

# COMPUTER

# DATABASE

_____

_____

_____

_____

_____

_____

_____

_____

_____

# Draw a line to the images that MATCH.

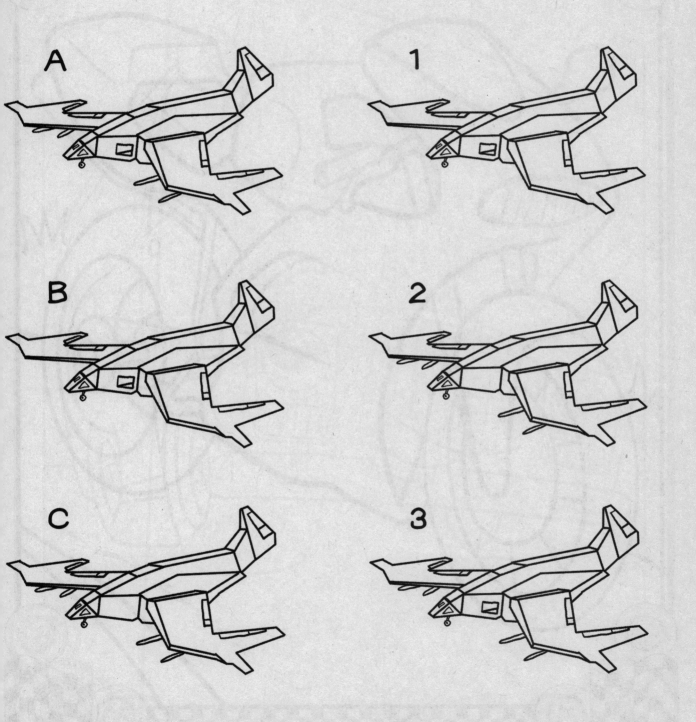

A

B

C

1

2

3

# Solve the MAZE

# FILL IN the missing letters.

1. I__AGI__AT__ON
2. D__EA__
3. __ELI__VE
4. C__E__TE
5. F__TU__E
6. __OV__R
7. O__TER S__A__E
8. __TA__S

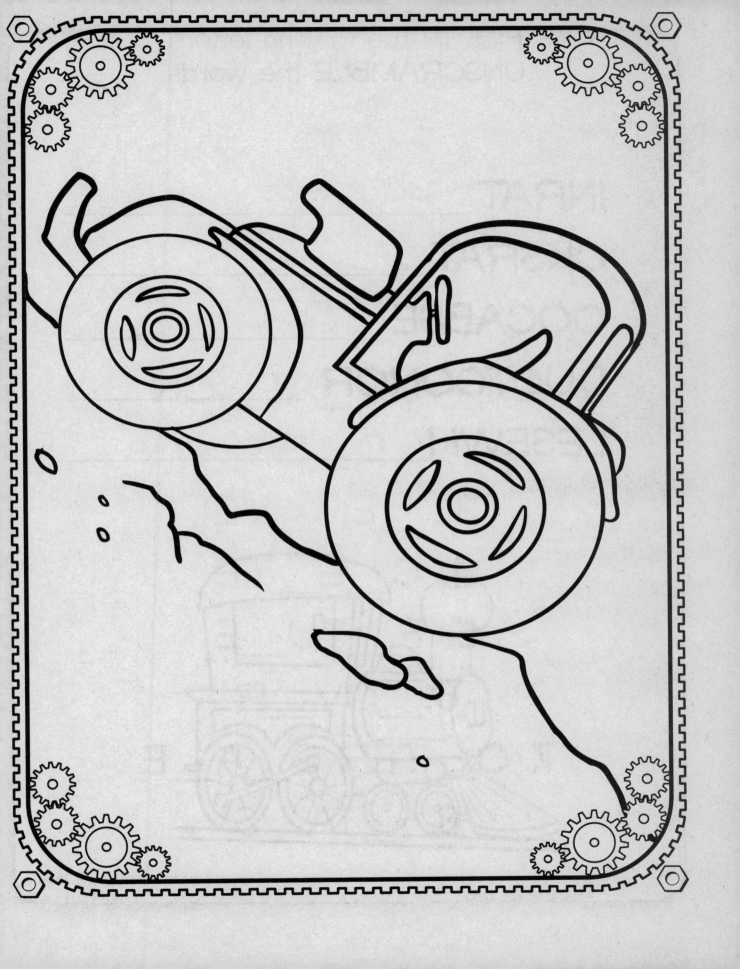

# UNSCRAMBLE the words.

INRAT _____

CKSRAT _____

OOCABSE _____

DUCTCONOR _____

LESEWH _____

# FIND and CIRCLE the words in the puzzle below:

SCOOTER    NAVIGATE

BICYCLE    GREEN

STREET     MOPED

VEHICLE    BRAKE

```
J G H U I B R A K E
T J Y M B M G J L A
S C O O T E R T O F
K H M P N W E S D S
O R B E B R E K S T
O C G D I E N O C R
J E L C I H E V Z E
P E Y B I C Y C L E
N A V I G A T E X T
```

# Circle the picture that is DIFFERENT.

A    B    C    D    E    F

# Connect the dots.

Use the grid
to help you
**DRAW**
the picture!

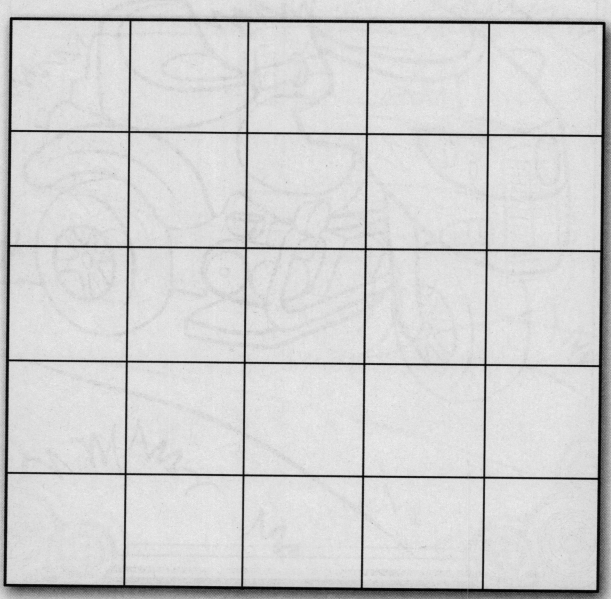

# Draw a line to the images that **MATCH**.

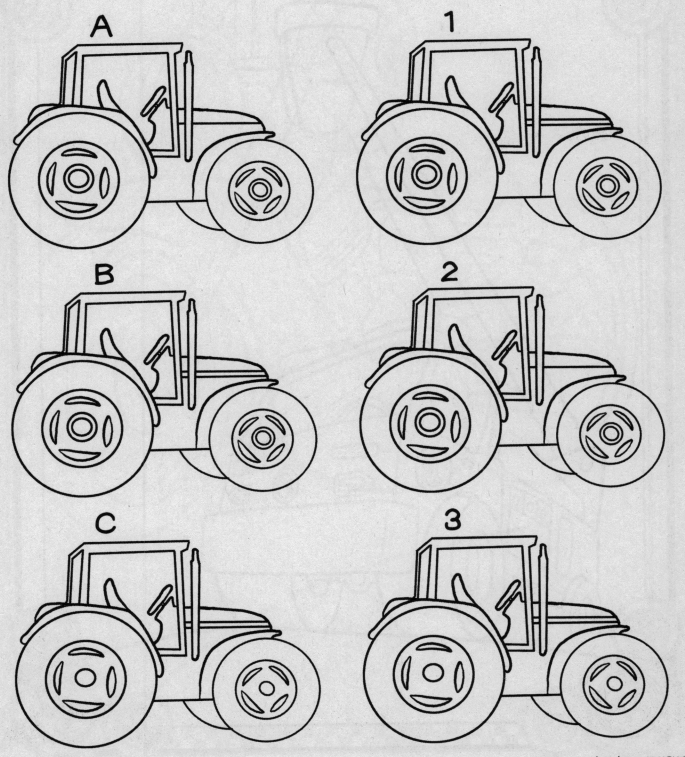

# Find the right path through the information super highway.

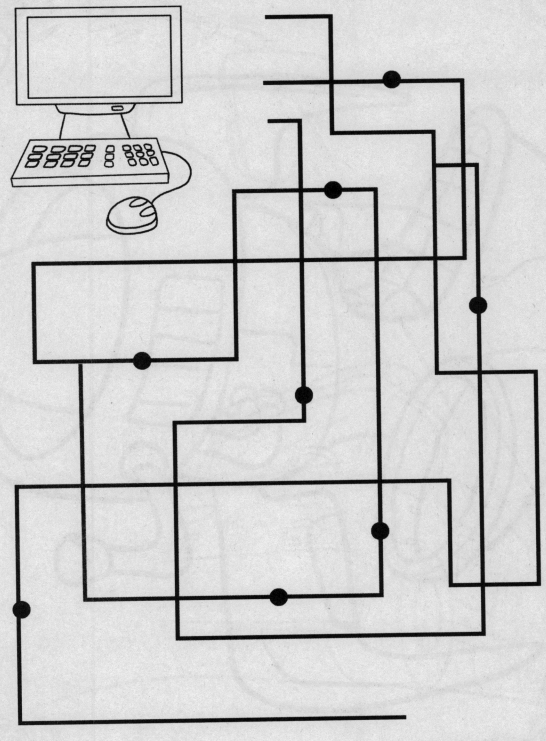

finish

# FIND and CIRCLE the words in the puzzle below:

RACECAR     SPEEDWAY

TRACK     FINISH LINE

ENGINE     SPEED

HUBCAPS     DRIVER

```
H U B C A P S D F I
O L P T R A C K U S
S P E E D N M D K P
W R T U E E D R Y E
F I N I S H L I N E
U T F K A R T V B D
O N E N G I N E N W
G T H C D B W R E A
R A C E C A R K T Y
```

# Circle the picture that is **DIFFERENT**.

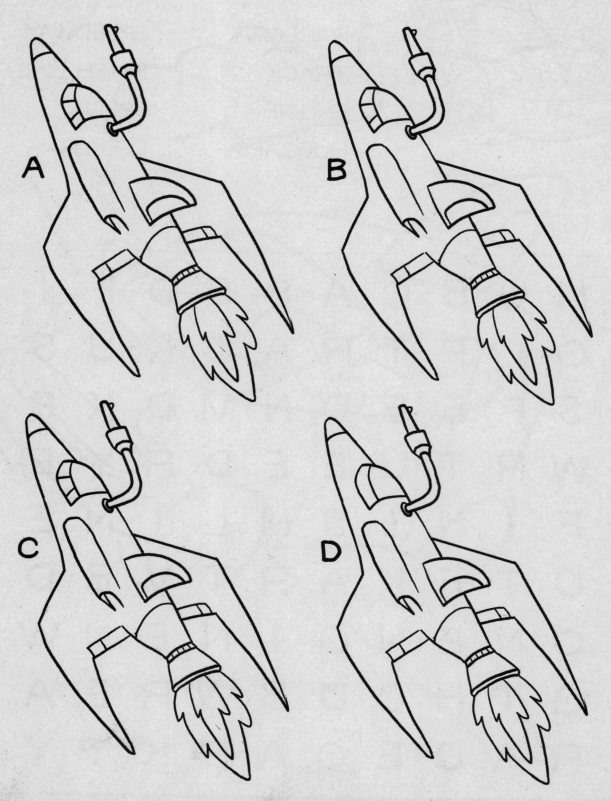

# Connect the dots.

Use the grid
to help you

**DRAW**

the picture!

# Solve the MAZE

start

finish

# FIND and CIRCLE the words in the puzzle below:

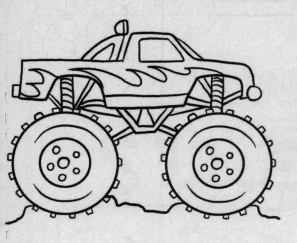

MONSTER      CLIMB

TRUCK      CRASH

DIRT      GIGANTIC

SMASH      TIRES

```
S N M O N S T E R T
L P O E E Z I G I D
C L I M B A R N J I
G T Z B T G E O U R
A C R A S H S L K T
G I G A N T I C A E
V H U Z D B X P T O
N W H S A M S O J R
H U X B N T R U C K
```

# WHICH TRUCK IS DIFFERENT?

# Solve the MAZE

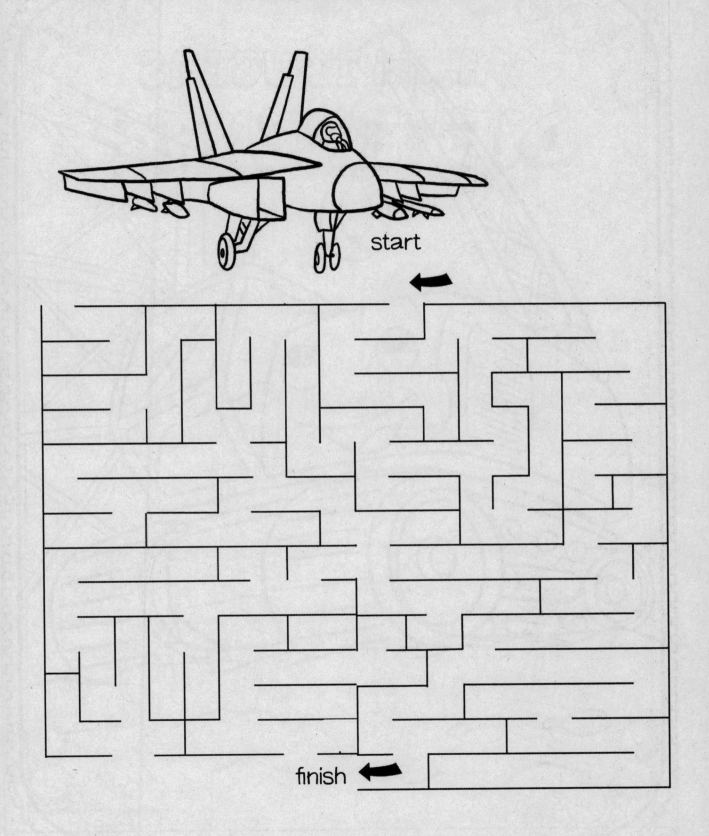

start

finish